LET'S VISIT PORTUGAL

Let's visit PORTUGAL

RONALD SETH

BURKE

First published September 1976
New revised edition 1984
© Ronald Seth 1976

ACKNOWLEDGEMENTS

The author and publishers are grateful to the following individuals and organisations for permission to reproduce photographs in this book:

Peter Baker; C. M. Dixon; the Portuguese Embassy and the Portuguese National Office.

The publishers also thank Garry Lyle for assistance in the preparation of this revised edition.

CIP data

Seth, Ronald
  Let's visit Portugal – 2nd ed.
  1. Portugal – Social life and customs – Juvenile literature
  I. Title
  946.9'042   DP532.7

  ISBN 0 222 01031 2

Burke Publishing Company Limited
Pegasus House, 116–120 Golden Lane, London EC1Y 0TL, England.
Burke Publishing (Canada) Limited
Registered Office: 20 Queen Street West, Suite 3000, Box 30, Toronto, Canada M5H 1V5.
Burke Publishing Company Inc.
Registered Office: 333 State Street, PO Box 1740, Bridgeport, Connecticut 06601, U.S.A.
Typeset in "Monophoto" Baskerville by Green Gates Studios Ltd., Hull, England.
Printed in Singapore by Tien Wah Press (Pte.) Ltd.

Contents

PORTUGAL

FRANCE

SPAIN

ATLANTIC

OCEAN

MEDITERRANEAN SEA

N. AFRICA

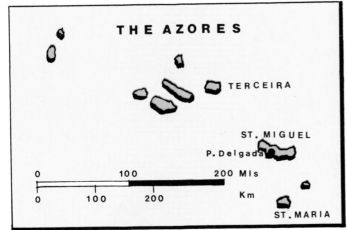

THE AZORES

TERCEIRA

ST. MIGUEL

P. Delgada

0	100	200 MIs
0	100	200

Km

ST. MARIA

MADEIRA

MADEIRA

Funchal

A seaside village on Portugal's Atlantic coast

The Oblong Country

When you have made allowances for the waves in its frontier with Spain, and the headlands and the few bays of its coastline, Portugal is almost a perfect oblong. It has an area of 88,500 square kilometres (34,170 square miles), or with the islands of the Azores and Madeira, which are usually included with the mainland of Portugal, 92,000 square kilometres (35,520 square miles).

Portugal's only neighbour is Spain. Together they form what is known as the Iberian Peninsula, Iberia being the name which the Ancient Greeks gave it.

The great rivers of Spain which flow east to west—among them the Douro, the Guadalquivir, the Ebro, the Gaudiana and the Tagus—all pass through Portugal to reach the sea. There are, however, a number of rivers which rise in Portugal. The longest of them is the Mondego, whose 209 kilometres (130 miles) contain not a drop of Spanish water.

As with the rivers, so with the mountains, most of which are the western ends of the great Spanish ranges. The highest Portuguese range is the Serra da Estrela—1,992 metres (6,535 feet) roughly in the centre of the country.

Portugal is bounded on the north and east by Spain, and on the west and south by the Atlantic Ocean. Its greatest length from north to south is 576 kilometres (358 miles); and at its broadest it is 227 kilometres (141 miles) across.

The eastern and central parts of the country are the region

of mountains and valleys. The coastal area is low and flat, except on the west bank of the River Tagus opposite Lisbon, the capital, and at Cape St Vincent, where the Serra de Monchique—900 metres (2,950 feet) comes up to the sea.

Because of its 800 kilometres (500 miles) of coastline, the climate of Portugal is temperate. Only in the deep sheltered valleys and the high mountain regions does the country begin to have temperatures approaching those of the extremes of central Spain. The most southern province, the Algarve, is sometimes called the "Land of Continuous Summer" though it can be cold, windy and wet for days on end.

About ten million people live in Portugal—an average of roughly 108 people to the square kilometre (0.4 square miles). This is much higher than the average figure for Spain.

Because of the mountainous interior of Portugal, the total length of the roads is not very high—about 35,000 kilometres (21,750 miles). The main roads, however, are very good. Even the secondary roads are rarely poor, by contrast with those of many European countries. Despite this comparatively small road system, all places of importance both to inhabitants and visitors are easy to reach by road.

Besides the roads, there are 3,588 kilometres (2,230 miles) of railway. This is broad-gauge, as in Spain, so there is no difficulty when passing by train from Spain to Portugal.

Portugal is divided into twenty-two administrative districts. Eighteen are in European Portugal, and the other four are in the Azores Islands and the island of Madeira. The Azores lie in the North Atlantic, some 1,450 kilometres (900 miles) west of Lisbon, while Madeira and its three little satellites lie about 800 kilometres (500 miles) south-west of Lisbon, off the west coast of Morocco.

The country is also divided into larger sections called provinces. These divisions are traditional and the Portuguese think of themselves as belonging to a particular province rather than to a particular administrative district.

The island of Madeira — cliffs of volcanic rock off the south-east coast

From Romans to Moors to Reconquest

The people who lived in the Iberian Peninsula before history began to be recorded, were among the earliest people to inhabit Europe. A skeleton of a man has been found not far from Gibraltar which, it is claimed, is 45,000 years old.

The Iberians were dark-skinned and thick-set, and there was no difference between those who lived in the regions now called Spain and Portugal. Because of its position, how-ever, "on the edge of the world" (Cape St Vincent was the "end of the earth" to the Greeks and Romans, because from there they could see the sun swallowed up by the sea) what we now know as Portugal attracted the trading nations of the Mediterranean—the Carthaginians, the Phoenicians, the Greeks and the Romans.

While they were building their great empire, the Romans were attracted to the Iberian Peninsula because it was so rich in olive oil and wine—still Portugal's two largest manufactures. Gaul had been quickly conquered and romanized. But the Roman Legions were to find that while what is now Spain put up little resistance, when they reached what is now northern Portugal they were to encounter a tribe called the Lusitanians who were not willing to surrender so easily. Not until their leader, Vitriatus, had been betrayed to the Romans and killed, did the Lusitanians accept the rule of Rome.

All this happened between 35 B.C. and 27 B.C.

The Romans regarded the Iberian Peninsula as one big

The Romans colonised the Iberian Peninsula and left their mark on Portuguese culture. These are the remains of a Roman temple

vineyard and olive grove. On this account they did not develop the area as they did Britain, Gaul and most of their other conquests. However, they did build a few roads, bridges and aqueducts. They also founded a few cities, of which nothing remains today but their names.

As the Roman Empire began to decline, Vandals and other Barbarian invaders discovered the Iberian Peninsula, and when these lost their power (round about A.D. 450 to 500) the chief tribe in Portugal, the Suebi, for a time set up an independent kingdom.

Two or three centuries earlier the first Christian missionaries had arrived in Iberia. They were given a warmer welcome there than they had been given anywhere. As early as the sixth century, i.e. A.D. 500 to A.D. 600, the Christian Church was dominant. Chapels and monasteries sprang up all along the banks of the Douro and Mondego rivers.

When the Visigoths swept through France and Spain in A.D. 585, the kingdom of the Suebi became part of Visigothic Spain. From this time until the invasion of the Moors from North Africa in A.D. 711 Portugal had no separate existence.

The Moors were able to conquer the peninsula fairly easily, because after the death of King Wamba of the Visigoths, the barons quarrelled among themselves and refused to join together to fight the invader. Not only that, the then king, Rodrigo, was betrayed to the Emir of Africa, so that there

Even today, in the Algarve, in southern Portugal, most of the houses are like square boxes. This is a result of the Moorish influence. Such houses are effective in keeping out the heat

was no all-powerful leader behind whom the barons could have rallied. All this enabled the Moors to march through the peninsula as far as Poitiers, in France.

The Moors were good masters. Under their rule, irrigation of the land was introduced, and orchards sprang up everywhere. Cities, white and fawn-coloured, came into being and prospered. The Moors welcomed the Jews and their business activities, and protected the Christian monasteries and their monks. But always the barons north of the Douro were waiting for the opportunity to drive the invaders from their country.

In the age of the Crusades, the younger sons of the great Portuguese families frequently left home to join the excitement of fighting in the Holy Land, or anywhere else where the Muslims, especially the Turks could be found. Some of them, however, felt that their first task should be to push the Moors out of their own country before going crusading.

In the second half of the eleventh century, Ferdinand I of Castile (part of Spain) and his successor Alfonso VI successfully drove the Moors south, to the other side of the River Tagus. The reconquered area was formed into a province, and given the name Porto Callo, from a Roman settlement called Porta Cale (the Cale Gate) which later became changed into Portugal.

In 1094, Alfonso VI gave the province of Portugal to his son-in-law, Count Henry of Portugal. When Henry died, his son was able to break away from the crown of Castile and

Léon and, when only twenty, had himself crowned king, as Alfonso I of Portugal.

Alfonso I kept up the war against the Moors, and eventually drove them still further south. He captured Lisbon and six other Moorish strongholds, and added them all to his kingdom of Portugal. In 1143, Castile recognised Portugal as an independent nation.

While all this fighting against the Moors was taking place, Portugal in some miraculous way, prospered. This was due chiefly to the efficiency of Alfonso I and his successors.

By the time Alfonso I's grandson, Sancho II, came to the throne at the age of thirteen, the Moors had been pushed further and further south until now they held only a small part of the province of the Algarve.

Unfortunately, the last years of Sancho's reign saw the outbreak of civil war in Portugal. This happened because Sancho seemed to have lost all authority and became unable to enforce the law. At all events, his brother Alfonso was given authority by the Pope to take over the government. Sancho naturally refused to give up the crown and he and his supporters fought Alfonso and his supporters.

In January 1248, after two years of civil war, Sancho died at Toledo, in Spain, and Alfonso declared himself king. Alfonso III proved to be a good ruler. He brought the divided Portuguese together, and drove the Moors out of the Algarve. What is known as the "Reconquest", that is, the final removal of the Moors, was complete.

The Golden Past

Alfonso III moved the capital of Portugal from Coimbra to Lisbon, which has been the capital of the country ever since. He also summoned the first National Assembly (the *Cortes*) at which ordinary men and women were represented.

Unfortunately, Alfonso's reign was not all a bed of roses. For some reason, while still married to the Countess Matilda of Boulogne, he decided to marry Princess Beatrice, daughter of Alfonso X of Castile. Naturally, the Church objected to this bigamous marriage, and the Pope excommunicated Alfonso. Alfonso refused to give up Princess Beatrice; in 1262 their marriage was, somewhat strangely, recognised by the Church.

Alfonso had no sons by Matilda of Boulogne, but he had a son, Diniz (Denis) by Beatrice. The recognition of his marriage to Beatrice meant that Denis could succeed him as king.

Denis proved to be as progressive as his father. During his reign (1279–1325) Portugal made close ties with western Europe; the first Portuguese university was founded; Portuguese literature came into being; and, most importantly, Portugal acquired a navy. (How important this was, we shall see presently.) Despite these advances, however, Denis became especially known as the Farmer King.

Though he was at heart a "peaceful king", his reign had its share of upsets. On several occasions he was at war with Castile; and, in the later years of his reign, he was troubled by the rebellious activities of his son, who was to become Alfonso

The tomb of Inez de Castro, with whom Pedro I was deeply in love. When she was murdered, he had her buried in a tomb opposite his own . . .

IV. The rebellion of Alfonso was encouraged by his mother, Isabella, daughter of Peter III of Aragon, who was later to become St. Elizabeth of Portugal.

During the reign of Alfonso IV war broke out between Portugal and Castile. Peace was made, however, when Alfonso agreed to fight with the army of Castile against the Moors, over whom they won a great victory on the Salado river in Andalusia, in Spain.

Alfonso was succeeded by his son Pedro, who married Constance, the daughter of the heir to the throne of Castile.

18

. . . so that when the Resurrection of the Dead took place, they would arise from the tomb face to face

Constance brought with her to Portugal a lady-in-waiting named Inez de Castro. Pedro fell violently in love with Inez, and they had two sons.

Pedro's love for Inez met with opposition from the Portuguese nobility and eventually she was assassinated. Pedro was beside himself with grief and gave orders that her body should be crowned and laid to rest in a tomb opposite his own, so that when the Resurrection of the Dead took place, they should come out of their graves face to face.

Pedro was a good king. He was chiefly interested in justice

19

and, though he ruled with an iron fist, the people were happy and the country prospered during his reign.

Pedro renewed the Portuguese claim to the throne of Castile. When he died, Ferdinand, his son by Constance, carried on the dispute with the other claimant, Henry of Trastamara. In 1369 Henry invaded Portugal. After two years of war, peace was made, by which Ferdinand gave up his claim to Castile, and promised to marry Henry's daughter. Instead, however, he married a Portuguese, Leonor Teles.

There was also another claimant to the throne of Castile. This was the Englishman, John of Gaunt (the father of King Henry IV) who had married Pedro's elder daughter. Ferdinand now made an alliance with John of Gaunt, which made Henry of Trastamara angry and he again invaded Portugal and besieged Lisbon. Again Ferdinand had to surrender, and this time Henry insisted that Ferdinand should break off the alliance with England.

After Henry's death, the alliance with England was resumed, when John of Gaunt's brother Edmund (later to become Duke of York) took an army to Portugal to help Ferdinand invade Castile. Ferdinand agreed to marry his daughter Beatrice to Edmund's son, but a little later he changed his mind, and instead she married King John I of Castile.

Ferdinand's strange behaviour over the marriage did not affect the alliance with England and, since 1380, with a break of only sixty years in the sixteenth century, Portugal and

Britain have been allies. This is the longest lasting alliance in the world.

Ferdinand died without an heir. His wife Leonor Teles became regent, while once again Castile claimed the Portuguese crown.

Quite a large number of Portuguese did not agree with the claim that the kings of Portugal made for the crown of Castile. They believed, with some reason, that these quarrels and wars were preventing the country from growing more prosperous. Unfortunately, Queen Leonor had long had a favourite, João, Count of Ourém, who was pro-Castile. Fearing that Leonor might be persuaded by the count to give Portugal to Castile, those who were anti-Castile chose John, one of Pedro's sons by Inez de Castro, to be their leader. John killed Ourém and, at the wish of the people of Lisbon, took the title of Defender of the Realm. Leonor eventually fled to Castile.

The struggle between Portugal and Castile was finally settled in August 1385. John I of Castile suddenly appeared in Portugal with a large army. The Portuguese army, led by John of Portugal, who had agreed to become king in the previous April, was only about half the size of the Castilian army. In spite of this, however, when the two armies met at Aljubarrota on 15th August, the Castilian army was soundly defeated. Many of the Castilian nobility were killed and the rest fled. John of Castile barely escaped with his life. At last, Portugal was safe.

A small force of English archers had taken part in the battle of Aljubarrota, and it was partly because of this that the alliance between England and Portugal was made binding by the Treaty of Windsor, signed on 9th May, 1386. A little later, John of Gaunt took an English army to Portugal and, with John of Portugal, attacked Castile again. This time Castile successfully beat off the invasion. However, King John married John of Gaunt's daughter, Philippa of Lancaster, who gave him four sons. In the same year, 1387, a truce was arranged with Castile which lasted for the next twenty-four years. In 1411, the two countries signed a peace treaty.

It might be thought that the constant struggle for so many years between Portugal and Castile would have prevented any improvement in the Portuguese way of life. Strangely this did

Because of the many battles between Portugal and her invaders, fortified castles are to be found in many areas. This is one of the castles at Sintra

not happen. By the time of the treaty of 1411, Portuguese commerce had prospered; however, from 1411 onwards it took even greater strides forward.

The alliance with England had been Portugal's only outside contact while she was busy keeping the Castilians out of the country. After the truce of 1387, however, Portugal had begun to look further afield for trade and found in Flanders a close trading friend. This was partly the result of the marriage of John's daughter Isabella to Philip the Good of Burgundy.

The real turning-point in Portugal's history, however, was 1415. From being a small country on the Iberian Peninsula, with a couple of overseas friends, she now began to develop into one of the world's great powers. In 1415 she seized Ceuta, in North Africa, opposite Gibraltar, from the Moors and thus acquired her first overseas territory.

A country with a coast-line as long as Portugal's almost automatically produces a nation of sea-farers, as does an island country, such as Britain. Before many years had passed, the fifteenth-century Portuguese were to become the greatest explorers of their time.

The great leader of Portuguese exploration was Prince Henry, one of the sons of John I and Philippa of Lancaster. He was known as "the Navigator" although, as a matter of fact, he never sailed further than Tangier, near Ceuta.

After the conquest of Ceuta, Prince Henry retired to a promontory at Sagres, in the Algarve. There he gathered round him experienced seamen, mapmakers and astronomers.

Together these scholars were the first to compile a guide to navigating the great oceans. At Sagres, too, a new kind of ship was built. Called a caravel, it had a broad beam and was so stoutly built that it could sail the seas in the roughest weather. (Columbus's ships were caravels.)

Having produced the theory of navigation, Henry decided to put it into practice, and with the help of the most expert seamen he could find, he organised voyages of exploration. His chief aim was to find a sea-route to India and the east. The trading caravans from the Orient, bringing precious stones, spices, silks and gold, were becoming more and more threatened by bandits along the overland trade routes, despite the fact that they paid heavy protection money. Henry argued that not only would a sea-route be safer, but that one ship would be able to carry the load of several caravans.

The first discovery made by Henry's sailors in 1419 was the island of Madeira, which lies off the west coast of Morocco. To the south of Madeira are the Canary Islands, which the Portuguese reached next. In the following few years attempts were made to settle Madeira and the Canaries, but without much success. The Azores, a group of islands some 1,450 kilometres (900 miles) out in the Atlantic, west of Portugal, were discovered some time between 1427 and 1431. Great efforts were then made to settle all three groups of islands with a mixture of Portuguese and Flemings (people from Queen Isabella's home country, Flanders).

Progress was slow but, after 1445 when it was found that

Fifteenth-century Portugal is famous for its voyages of exploration. Some of the remains of fifteenth-century buildings are witness to other skills. This amazing aqueduct is at Elvas

sugar would grow well there (which made the islands very important to Portugal) more and more settlers began to arrive.

While this was taking place, Prince Henry's ships were probing the coast of Africa. In 1434, they passed Cape Bojador, 320 kilometres (200 miles) south of the Canaries, and Rio de Oro, another 400 kilometres (250 miles) further south, two years later.

A lighter caravel was now brought into service. In these ships Arguin was reached in 1444; and, in 1446, another expedition sailed 210 kilometres (130 miles) past Cape Verde. Henry, however, did not live to see the discovery of the sea-route to India. When he died in 1460 the equator had still to be crossed.

King Alfonso V, who had succeeded to the throne in 1483, was more interested in military conquests than in voyages of discovery. In 1458, 1461 and 1471 he sent expeditions against Morocco; the first two were unsuccessful, but the last captured Tangier and Arzila.

Though the African discoveries were not completely neglected, it was not until the reign of John II (1481–1495) that there were new voyages of discovery. John's ambition was to make Portugal not just a country "on the edge of the world", but an important European power. He had the firm belief that this would be best achieved by turning Portugal into a great trading nation.

In the very first year of his reign, he gave orders for a fortified trading-post to be set up without delay at Elmina, in the Gulf of Guinea. At the same time, he made money and ships available for further voyages of discovery. No time was lost and, in the second year of John's reign, Diego Cão discovered the mouth of the Congo River. Continuing south, four years later, in 1486, he reached Cape Cross, half-way down what is now called South West Africa, or Namibia.

All these early expeditions paved the way for the first great success. In 1488, Henry the Navigator's dream came true when Bartholomeu Diaz rounded the Cape of Storms, the southernmost tip of Africa, which he renamed the Cape of Good Hope.

Then, in 1492, Christopher Columbus, who had lived in Madeira for some years and had become interested in navigation, returned from an expedition across the Atlantic. He had made this voyage on behalf of the Spanish king and queen, and he returned with the news that he had discovered the Indies. Naturally, this very much upset the Portuguese, though when Columbus made no mention of the spiceries and cities of the east, they began to believe that he had not discovered the Indies at all. They were right; he had accidentally discovered America.

Determined to be the first to reach the Indies by sea, John II ordered an expedition to be prepared to sail for India. In July 1497 Vasco da Gama set sail with four ships. They reached Calicut on the west coast of India (not to be confused with Calcutta) in the spring of 1498, and they returned to Lisbon in the autumn of 1499 with cargoes of eastern merchandise.

This encouraged the Portuguese to even greater activity. In 1500 Pedro Cabral discovered Brazil and claimed it for Portugal. But it was the east, via the Cape of Good Hope, that attracted them most. This was because of the rich trade that the east could provide.

Within the next few years Portuguese explorers and merchants were the first white men to reach Indonesia, China, Japan and Australia. Some of them became the first men to sail round the world (in 1519–22). At the same time, others were setting up trading-posts and colonies in Africa —in Angola on the west coast, and at Lourenço Marques in what was to become the colony of Mozambique on the east coast; in India, at Goa, which became the capital of the Portuguese eastern empire; at Malacca, in what is now western Malaysia; in the Moluccas, in modern Indonesia; and at Macao, on the coast of China, opposite Hong Kong.

For a period of more than fifty years Portugal was one of the richest countries in Europe. She had an overseas empire larger even than that of Spain (which had laid claim to South America with the exception of Brazil, which Portugal had discovered). Unfortunately, the riches brought out the worst in the Portuguese. Their great qualities of endurance, seriousness and tolerance were replaced by a life of luxurious idleness.

Then a king called Sebastian came to the throne. He was only three when he succeeded his grandfather in 1557. Even while he was still quite a young boy he became determined to organise a crusade against Morocco, and for some years he spent all his energies getting together men and arms. By 1578 he felt that his preparations were complete. Placing himself at the head of his forces, he crossed into Morocco in June. On 4th August he joined battle with the Moorish army.

The result was a catastrophe for Portugal. Sebastian's forces were utterly defeated. He himself was killed together with eight thousand of his men, while another fifteen thousand were taken prisoner. The tragedy was that the great defeated army represented all the best of Portuguese manhood.

Sebastian, who had no children, was succeeded by his great-uncle Henry. Henry was a cardinal and was therefore forbidden to marry. He was also the last surviving member of the royal family.

The central courtyard of the palace of the Dukes of Braganza

On the death of Henry, Philip II of Spain, who was the nephew and son-in-law of John III of Portugal, claimed the Portuguese throne. At first, the Portuguese refused to recognise him as king, but in 1581 he sent the Duke of Alva to Portugal on his behalf and all opposition to Spanish rule collapsed.

For the next sixty years Portugal was ruled by Spain. From time to time the Portuguese protested. Twice they rebelled, only to be defeated. Then, in 1640, a strong leader was found in the Duke of Braganza. At the head of another revolution, Duke John drove the Spaniards from Portugal. Fifteen days later, on 15th December, he was crowned John IV. However, it was not until 1668 that the Spaniards at last recognised their neighbour as an independent country.

John IV further strengthened Portugal's ties with England by marrying his daughter Catherine to the English king Charles II. Her dowry consisted of the gift of Bombay and Tangier to England, in return for which Charles promised to provide men and arms to help the Portuguese in their struggle against Spain.

These wars with Spain were very expensive in manpower and money. Because the strength of the armies had to be kept up, the necessary number of men could not be spared to look after trade in the faraway empire, and this meant that money was not available for other things besides war. However, this situation changed with the discovery in Brazil of gold in 1692 and diamonds in 1713. From this time on Brazil provided Portugal with most of her wealth.

During the reign of John V (1706–1750) the country enjoyed a prosperity which it had not known since before the conquest by Spain. The king took for himself one-fifth of all the riches that came from Brazil, which meant that he did not have to ask parliament to vote him money. In time he stopped summoning parliament. And, since he himself was not really interested in governing, he put the government of the country in the hands of ministers. What he was interested in was using his wealth to obtain honours for himself—he gave money to the Pope so that he might have the title of His Most

30

Faithful Majesty, and also so that the Archbishop of Lisbon should be called the Patriarch of Portugal.

Such things did nothing for the Portuguese people; they only satisfied the king's vanity. However, John did use some of his money wisely by founding academies and libraries.

Unhappily, in the second half of his reign, the ministers he appointed to govern Portugal were not equal to their task. As a result, the country declined in every way. Rather than going forward, it first stood still, and then began to go back.

When John died in 1750, his son Joseph realized how low the country had sunk. He appointed as his chief minister Sebastio Carvalho, who was later to become the Marquis of Pombal. He could not have made a wiser choice.

Pombal was a clever man. He made strict regulations for the diamond trade, so that too many of the precious stones should not be sold at once, thus keeping their price high; and he controlled the production and sale of sugar. He also started a national silk industry; formed one company to control the sardine and tunny fishing; and formed another company to trade with Brazil.

He reached the height of his power after the great earthquake in November 1755, which destroyed two-thirds of Lisbon. There was widespread panic but Pombal remained cool, directed all the rescue operations and then planned the rebuilding of the capital.

By treaties made in 1654 and 1661, English merchants had been given special rights in Portugal. Less than a hundred years later, the English practically controlled Portugal's trade. Pombal set up a Board of Trade to keep the activities of the English merchants within bounds, and a General Company for Wine Culture to control the port wine trade. He formed companies for the manufacture of hats and cutlery, among other things. He also reformed the University of Coimbra and established primary education in Portugal.

In doing all these things to benefit his country, Pombal made many enemies among people who were jealous of him. When King Joseph died these enemies persuaded his successor, Maria I, to remove Pombal and try him for a number of so-called crimes. Fortunately for him, his greatest enemy, the Queen Mother Marianne Victoria, died; and all that happened to him was that he was forbidden to live within forty kilometres (twenty-five miles) of the Court.

Once again war broke out with Spain, and Portugal called on the British for help. Peace was made in 1777. When Spain declared war on France (ruled by Napoleon) in 1793, both Portugal and England went to the aid of Spain. Spain made a separate peace two years later, which left Portugal still at war with France until she, too, signed a peace treaty at Amiens in 1802. England remained at war with France until Napoleon was defeated finally in 1815.

For the next five years, Portugal was left in peace. Then Napoleon, who had already invaded Spain, demanded the surrender of Portugal. Maria I had become mad after reigning for only a few years, and her son, John, took over the government as Prince Regent. When the French armies entered Portugal, Prince John and other members of the Royal Family boarded ships of a British fleet commanded by Sir Sydney Smith, which was lying in the Tagus, and were taken to Brazil.

In August 1808, a British army under the command of Sir Arthur Wellesley (later Duke of Wellington) arrived in Portugal. For the next six years there was a fierce war between the British-Portuguese forces and those of Napoleon. It ended with the defeat of the French in 1814.

This war caused great destruction in Portugal, and there was much discontent among the people. Prince John, now king, showed no desire to return from Brazil until he was compelled to do so. In Portugal, there had been a revolution which set up a council of army officers to rule the country. This council was overthrown in 1824, and it was then that John decided to leave Brazil—which he had already made an independent country—and return to Portugal.

The history of Portugal for the next three-quarters of a century is one of political unrest, with various parties struggling against the crown. These struggles came to a head in 1910 with a revolution organised by the Republican Party which succeeded in overthrowing the monarchy. King Manuel II managed to escape to Gibraltar and from there to England. He lived for some years in Twickenham, on the River Thames, not far from London but when he died, in 1932, his body was returned to Portugal.

Although Portugal still possessed her overseas empire, since

Vasco da Gama's arrival in India in 1498 a number of other European countries had acquired empires: the Spaniards in South America and Africa, the Dutch in the Orient and the West Indies, the Germans in Africa, and the British whose empire was so widespread throughout the world that the sun never set on it.

These and other empires took away much of Portugal's importance as a world power. In fact, Portugal's Golden Age was the fifty years or so during which Portuguese navigators opened up the sea-routes of the world by their fearless voyages of discovery.

Many Farms and Some Factories

Over half the people of Portugal make their living on the land. Except in the mountainous regions, the soil is very fertile, but agricultural methods are out-dated, and much of the land that could be cultivated is still neglected.

Oxen are still chiefly used for agricultural work and for some of the transport in the country districts, while the donkey is most used for carrying loads. The ox-carts have solid wheels, and ploughs are made of the branches of trees; neither have changed since the time the Romans were in Portugal, nearly two thousand years ago. Where the land is irrigated, the irrigation machinery is similar to that used by the Moors, a thousand years ago.

Oxen, traditional beasts of burden in Portugal, drawing a plough

Over one-fifth of all Portugal is forest. There is a large variety of trees, among them the pine, the oak, the chestnut and the cork oak.

Portugal is the greatest producer of cork in the world. In fact, more cork is grown in Portugal than in all the rest of the world put together.

Wheat is the most widely grown crop. Since the beginning of the century, however, the Portuguese have eaten more wheat than any other cereal. They can never grow enough, and so have to import the balance from other countries.

Olive trees are found all over Portugal. The oil which they produce is the second most valuable crop; indeed, Portugal has now become one of the world's largest producers of olive oil.

Grapes are grown over most of northern and central Portugal. The most valuable wine which is made from these grapes is port wine, which has been the country's chief export for several centuries. However, besides port, which is an after-dinner wine, table wines, which are drunk during a meal, are also produced. Quite large quantities of these table wines are exported to Portuguese-speaking countries, and in recent years there has been a steady export of very light table wines, known because of their pale red colour as *rosé*, to America and Europe, especially to Britain.

In valleys where there are several rivers, which make it possible to form paddy-fields, rice is grown. It might seem strange to find rice being grown in Europe, because one mostly thinks of rice needing the hot, damp climate of the east. Admittedly, the quantity grown in Portugal is not very large, but that it is grown at all is a sign of the Portuguese willingness to be adventurous about their crops, if not about their equipment.

Fruit is grown throughout Portugal. The crop is large enough to supply Portugal's own needs and to provide a surplus which is exported either as fresh fruit or in the form of candied or preserved fruits.

Other Portuguese agricultural products include barley, oats, rye and maize. The most southern province, the Algarve, is world-famous for its almonds and figs, while Setúbal is almost as famous for oranges and Elvas for plums.

Gathering the grape harvest

The pine forests are also a valuable source of income. Pit-props and turpentine are made from these trees, as is resin. The extraction of resin was begun about fifty years ago; by the end of the Second World War, resin had become Portugal's fourth most important export.

Many sheep are reared in the east of Portugal. Pigs and mules are bred in the Alentejo, which is also the home of the fighting bulls. Some cattle are also raised, but sheep and goats by far outnumber them.

All along the coasts of Portugal there are fishing villages and a fishing fleet leaves Lisbon every year for Newfoundland to fish for cod. Most of the fish is eaten by the Portuguese themselves, but there is a big export trade in sardines, which are prepared and canned at Setúbal and at Matozinhos, near

37

A flock of sheep with typical farm buildings in the background

Oporto. Tunny is caught off the south coast of the Algarve, and some of this is exported too.

When it is remembered over half of the people make their living on the land, it comes as no surprise that Portuguese industries are not very extensive. What there are, are mostly connected with the preparation of products for export; for example, the manufacture of cork and of glass for wine bottles; and good quality textiles which are made from home-grown wool, or cotton imported from the ex-colonies. One industry which is truly Portuguese is the manufacture of *azulejos*— beautiful porcelain tiles, which have been made since the days of the Moors. Most of the industries are to be found in and around Lisbon and other large cities.

Portugal is very rich in coal but at the present time not much of it is mined. There are also fairly extensive deposits of valuable minerals, which include tin, copper, wolfram, manganese, lead and kaolin. The country made a considerable fortune during the Second World War by selling some of these minerals, especially wolfram, or tungsten (used in making electric light bulbs and radio valves) to both the Allies and Germany, who bid against one another for them.

As with Spain, so with Portugal, tourism has become an important source of income since the Second World War. The centre of tourism is the most southern province, the Algarve, which is said by some to have continual summer, though this is not strictly true.

A fisherman at Setúbal unloading his catch. Note his special wide-brimmed hat

There is an airport at Faro, the capital of the Algarve, and from Faro the resorts along the coast can be reached by train, bus or car.

From Faro itself, eastwards through Tavira to Vila Real de Santo Antonio, and westwards through Loulé, Albufeira and Lagoa to Lagos is an almost continuous beach. In what were once quiet little fishing villages, hotels, holiday flats, clubs and bars have sprung up. Fortunately the building has been better controlled and planned than in the great holiday centres of Spain, the Costa Brava and the Costa del Sol. The hotels are not huge, but many of them are modern, comfortable and even luxurious, with swimming-pools and other tourist attractions.

Modern Portugal

The new republic's history during its first twenty years was as unsettled as the last two or three hundred years of the monarchy had been. The political parties which had come into being could not agree on the best way to govern the country. There were revolutions and counter-revolutions, and it was said that in Portugal you could never go to bed and be sure that the same government would be in power when you woke up.

The longer the unsettled conditions lasted, the poorer the country became. The colonies no longer produced the rich trade which they had formerly brought to the Mother Country, and without this income modern industries could not be set up.

During the First World War (1914–1918) Portugal honoured its alliance with Britain, and troops were sent to fight against the Germans in the colonies in Africa.

After the war, the political situation in Portugal got worse instead of better. Leaders were assassinated and government followed government, most of which did not last longer than a few months. This state of affairs continued until 1928, when General Antonio Carmona was elected president after a particularly bloody revolution in the previous year.

By this time, as was only to be expected, the financial state of the country was very serious, and the government decided to ask the League of Nations for a loan. The League of Nations, however, would not grant a loan unless it controlled the way in which the money was spent. Somewhat naturally, the Portuguese objected to this and President Carmona called on Professor Antonio Salazar to be Minister of Finance, and try to sort out the country's financial problems. From this time until shortly before his death, Salazar and Portugal were one and the same.

Now why should President Carmona call on a professor of law at Coimbra University to solve the financial difficulties of his country?

Antonio Salazar was an extraordinary man. Though a lawyer, he had always been interested in economics; at one time he had been professor of economic sciences at Coimbra. Probably more interested in economics than the law, he had begun to write about economics, and in time these writings not only became widely known, but were recognised as coming from a real expert. In fact, he came to be regarded as the leading economic expert in Portugal.

It was not surprising, then, that the President should ask him to try to get Portugal out of her financial difficulties. Salazar would only agree to do so provided he could have an absolutely free hand, not only in financial matters, but in the organisation of government.

At first Salazar was just a powerful Minister of Finance. In 1932, however, he became Prime Minister. In fact, he became the government. The President was reduced to a figure-head, and the other members of the government did what Salazar told them to do.

Salazar never married and, though he was so powerful, he very rarely appeared in public. Whether this was deliberate or not, for the Portuguese he became a living legend.

At the same time, however, he began to put Portugal on a sound economic footing again. Unfortunately, this was done at the expense of the freedom of the individual. Salazar ruled Portugal with a rod of iron.

But, however much we may dislike dictatorship, it has to be admitted that Salazar prevented Portugal from becoming an out-cast in Europe. He also made Portugal financially sound and much respected as a trading country.

During the Second World War (1939–1945), Salazar found a way of remaining neutral and yet observing the spirit of the six-hundred-year-old alliance with Britain. Lisbon became a centre for both British and German espionage.

After the war, when all the other colonial powers were granting independence to their colonies, Salazar refused to do so. India, however, began to talk about "liberating" Goa and the settlements of Dadra, Nagar-Halevi, Daman and Diu in 1954. When Salazar would not negotiate with India, India broke off relations with Portugal. Not wishing to go to war, India organised peaceful mass "invasions" of Goa and the other settlements, but these were unsuccessful in persuading the inhabitants to accept Indian rule. Eventually, India lost patience. In December 1961 she sent an army into the territories and seized them, making them part of India. Until

To these children walking in a cobbled street of old Lisbon, Antonio Salazar is just a name. In fact, he was the most well-known Portuguese of the twentieth century

1975, Portugal kept all her colonies, but she has now given independence to all but one.

Salazar was also responsible for the way in which Portugal is governed. In 1933 he introduced what he called the New State. At the head of the country is the President, elected for seven years. The President appoints the Prime Minister and some of the other Ministers. The old *cortes* (parliament) was replaced by two bodies; one, the National Assembly of deputies, is elected democratically every four years; the other is the Consultative Assembly, made up of members of the trades and professions. In Salazar's days, both bodies were really rubber stamps, who were expected to—and did—pass all the laws proposed by the dictator.

Salazar allowed a little opposition, but anyone voting for the opposition was likely to have an unwelcome visit from the secret police. Salazar's party, the National Union, always won all the seats in the National Assembly.

In 1968, Salazar had a stroke and was no longer able to govern. He died on 27th July 1970. Until 1974, his successors were able to carry on in much the same way as Salazar but, in April of that year, the Armed Forces revolted and overthrew the government. Long months of experiment followed, during which there were disagreements among the leaders of the revolt themselves, and between the army and the political parties, which had come out of hiding. However, the country now appears to be settling down under a freely elected government.

44

Everyday Life, Customs and Pastimes

The Portuguese are a very serious people. This is not surprising because for most of their history they have had to struggle to make a living. On the other hand, they are not a sad people, though their gaiety is not expressed in the same way as the Spaniards express theirs—with singing, the continual music of guitars and much laughter. They have a gift for happiness, but it is a kind of serious happiness.

Despite this, the Portuguese enjoy themselves. Go to a country fair—*feira*—in any part of the country, and you will see how true this is. Each region has its own costumes, its own songs and dances. The gaily coloured material of both the men's and the women's costumes and the use of thousands and thousands of brightly coloured flowers as decoration, produce the right atmosphere for the merrymaking.

The Portuguese is never casual. If he is going to visit a friend he will put on a clean shirt, and he would never go to express his sorrow at a death without putting on black clothes. He is also very hospitable. Even the poorest family will insist that a visitor, even if he is a stranger, stays to have a meal.

The Portuguese loves to invite you into his house and, having got you there, will be reluctant to let you go. He will press all kinds of gifts on you, and will be seriously offended if you try to refuse them.

When you have a meal with a family, you do not begin to eat until your host urges you to. When it is over, if you are

Folk dancing in traditional costume in the Ribatejo. Each region has its own distinctive costumes

female you go and kiss your hostess, if male you kiss her hand, to thank her for going to all the trouble of preparing the meal.

The Portuguese kiss a great deal. Most Europeans kiss their female friends and relatives in greeting, but in Portugal it is not just a polite greeting, it is a sincere gesture of respect. A boy kisses the hand of his mother and grandmother, as a man kisses the hand of his wife and her women friends, out of respect for her as mother, wife or woman.

If you like tasting new kinds of food, then Portugal is the place for you. Even the Portuguese will agree with you that their meat is not very good, but they make up for this by many other exciting dishes. Naturally, olive oil is used a great deal in the preparation of food.

46

At festivals and fairs, and at parties in private houses, you will always be served *canja*. This is chicken broth in which rice is boiled with chopped chicken livers and gizzard. On non-party occasions instead of *canja* you are most likely to be given *cosido*, which is also a chicken broth, but it has far more fat in it, and is flavoured with a sprig of mint. Fish and other seafood, hare and rabbit are also used for making soups.

If it is at all possible, you must not miss *caldo verde* which is a favourite soup in the Minho, in the north, and *acordas* which is equally popular in the Alentejo, the province west of the River Tagus.

Caldo verde is made of thinly shredded cabbage cooked in a clear potato soup with slices of dry and rather spicy sausage. Pieces of corn-bread are floated in it to give it body. Eaten with a spoon and fork, it is often served at the *end* of a meal, to make certain that the guest cannot possibly be hungry.

Acordas is rather like a porridge. It is made from wheat-bread dipped in oil and flavoured with garlic and seasoned with herbs to which white fish and soft-boiled eggs are added. It may sound difficult to digest, but it is not. Delicate babies are often brought up on it.

The Alentejo also has a *gaspacho*, which is served iced, and is not unlike the Spanish *gaspacho*. It is made of bread soaked in vinegary water, to which tomatoes, cucumber, onions and green peppers are added. It is served with *croutons*, little squares of fried or toasted bread.

The course following the soup is usually memorable. It can

be a dish of rice to which mussels, or tunny, or chicken, or rabbit, or just tomatoes and peppers are added; or it can be meat or fish rissoles, stuffed pancakes or fritters.

At one time, hardly a Portuguese meal was ever without a dish of crayfish. Nowadays they are scarce and, because of the high price they fetch, most are exported. Stuffed crabs and shrimps are still popular.

Because of Portugal's long coast-line, fish of all kinds—except crayfish and the oyster (which has also disappeared)—is plentiful. There is sole, bass, brill, hake, red mullet, sword-fish, tunny, eel and, of course, sardines.

If you are ever in the Algarve, you must also try *ja cataplana*. This is cockles, served with sausages and bacon.

The fish most eaten, however, is cod. The Portuguese call it their "faithful friend" and it appears on the table in rich and poor houses alike several times a week. Fortunately, there are over three hundred ways of preparing cod; the most popular way is boiling it and serving it with cabbage, sprouts, turnips, onions, potatoes and a hard-boiled egg.

Portuguese beef is not usually tender enough to be eaten as steak, but there are several tasty dishes made of beef, served with mustard sauce and port wine, in a hot earthenware dish. There is often a fried egg perched on top of it.

Veal is never good in Portugal, because the Portuguese will not kill their calves young enough. This can be said of lamb and mutton, too, but not for the same reason. Because grazing for the sheep is too poor, they remain thin and their meat is

48

tough and has too much fat. But, by cooking for a long time in one or other of the traditional sauces, a reasonable dish can be made. Pork, on the other hand, is really good. Pigs are mostly bred in the cork and oak forests of the Alentejo, where they feed on acorns and white truffles.

Almost every dish you eat in Portugal is served with rice or fried potatoes, or both. The only salads are lettuce, tomato and green peppers.

The Portuguese love sweet dishes. The most popular dish is caramel cream, which is known as "365", because it appears on most Portuguese tables every day of the year. Portuguese housewives guard their sweet recipe-books as closely as the Bank of England used to guard over gold.

Marzipan is very popular. In the Alentejo and the Algarve, it is fashioned into all kinds of objects—animal, vegetable and mineral—with all the skill and care of a sculpture.

Much fresh fruit is eaten, and crystallised fruits, which are a luxury elsewhere, are cheap in Portugal.

Although most Portuguese drink "the wine of their region", beer is brewed, though it is not very strong. The best comes from Sagris. There are also a number of mineral waters, the most popular come from Castelo and Carvelhelhos.

Whether in the cities or the countryside, the family is the centre of Portuguese life. Usually it will be a large one, made larger still by stretching out to embrace far-distant relatives, even so far as cousins-in-law. The young and old are most respected. I have watched a great-granddaughter stand by her great-grandmother, holding a plate of food for over an hour, while the old woman slowly ate. Many middle-aged men will not smoke in front of their father if the father disapproves of smoking. On parents' birthdays and at Christmas the whole family must be together, usually at the house of the eldest member.

This love of family is probably the reason why most Portuguese do not like eating in restaurants. They would rather entertain in their homes, except on very special occasions, or when they have guests who would like to hear *fados*— traditional folk-songs, which are similar to the *flamencos* of Spain. Unfortunately, the art of the *fado* seems to be dying out, but it is possible to hear these fascinating songs in tourist restaurants in Lisbon and the other large cities, especially Coimbra, where the University students have their own *fados*.

Not so very long ago, whole families consisting of children, daughters-in-law, sons-in-law, grandparents and maiden aunts all crowded into one house. Nowadays, the young Portuguese woman is struggling to have a house of her own. Gradually she is winning, and this means that she will be less under the eye of older women, likely to be scolded if she does something of which they do not approve. When, in the past, girls spent much of their time on make-up, dress and shopping, now they meet boys in class, at the swimming-pool and on the tennis court. All this, of course, means that the Portuguese woman, at least in the cities, is becoming freer, but it is very

In country districts life has changed very little. These women are doing their weekly washing in the river

doubtful whether Women's Lib will go far in Portugal within the next fifty years.

In the country, the situation is changing very little, if at all. Women have always done their share of work in the fields, and still do. Girls have never been allowed to be alone with boys, even when courting, and this is still the case. But, as they have been brought up like this, and their mothers before them, the Portuguese girls accept it as normal. In any case, there are many opportunities at fairs, *romarias* (religious festivals) and pilgrimages for a boy and girl to slip away quietly for a quick kiss, without being missed by the usually watchful eyes of the grown-ups.

Beautiful flower arrangements—no two are the same—at the festival at Tomar, not far from Lisbon

As the family is at the centre of everyday life, so religion plays a chief part in the life of the individual. Though other religions are allowed so long as they do not upset law and order, the majority of Portuguese are Roman Catholics, as they have been for fifteen hundred years.

The Spaniards, who have been Roman Catholics, too, for as long as the Portuguese, have centred their religion on the agony of Christ. The Portuguese, in contrast, celebrate the happier side of Christ's life. Their gayest festival is Christmas; and though, naturally, they observe Easter with great solemnity, the Christ Child represents to the Portuguese the heart of a religion which they believe should stress human kindness and tenderness rather than spiritual piety.

Of course, they see Christ as the centre of their religion, but it is the Virgin Mary who really plays the leading part. Every village has its Virgin patroness, and there is great rivalry among the villages to make their image of the Virgin better than any other Virgin in the country. Her name, Maria, is burnt into pottery and painted on boats and carts; every woman embroiders it somewhere on her clothes and writes it in cinnamon on bread.

The saints and the angels are also treated as close friends. If you lose something, St. Anthony will help you find it; if you are anxious about getting your daughter married, he will find a husband for her. St. Peter watches over fishermen; St. Gonzalo finds husbands for old maids; St. Sebastian is the patron saint of artillery, while others watch over hunchbacks, thieves and stammerers, or save you from fire or illness.

Every saint has his "day" and on this day he will be honoured with a *romaria*, or festival. His statue is taken from the church and carried round the village, garlanded or pelted with flowers, to the music of the village band. When the religious part of the festival is over, the rest of the day is given up to feasting, singing and dancing. Practically everyone wears the costume of the region at a *romaria*.

Naturally, the *romaria* for the Virgin is the most splendid. In several parts of Portugal she is carried from village to village. For example, the image of Our Lady of Nazaré is carried round seventeen villages and in each village she stays a year, while Our Lady of Cabo makes the rounds of thirty-six villages, staying a year in each. The image is carried in a coach accompanied by the priests, while the coach is surrounded and guarded by images of angels. Crowds of people take part in the processions. At the *romaria* at Santa Eufemia, for instance, there are seldom less than 30,000 people.

With so many saints and so many Virgins, no one is likely to go to Portugal without being caught up in a *fiesta* or a *romaria*. You will be made as welcome as though you were a Portuguese.

But it is not just the Christ Child, the Virgin and the saints who receive all the honour. The Portuguese believe that God made water, fire and sunlight for man's enjoyment; and to thank God for them, they are honoured too. Tremendous patience and skill are devoted to making lamps for homes as well as shrines, and lanterns for ships and barns. Perhaps no more elaborate fountains are to be found anywhere than in Portugal, and water-containers of all kinds are fashioned and decorated to give thanks for it.

**A procession on
Good Friday, at Faro,
in the Algarve**

The hearth represents the heart of the home. The older members of the family have their seats close to it to warm their ancient bones; hams are smoked over the fire; peas and chestnuts are dried in it and then dough for the bread is stood by it to rise. The pokers, rakes and tongs are shaped like animals, both real and imaginary, and the pots and pans have been fashioned with loving care. In many of the villages a young man proposes by giving his chosen girl a set of miniature pots and pans, by which he is telling her that he is giving her his heart.

But the key to Portuguese life is three words—*se Deus quizer* ("if God wills"). "I will return at five o'clock, *se Deus quizer*,"—"Let us go to the cinema tomorrow, *se Deus quizer*,"—"I shall finish the book this week, *se Deus quizer*"—and when the radio announcer closes down and he wishes his listeners a goodnight, he adds, *se Deus quizer*.

Probably what most strikes the visitor from the busy, noisy world of the more industrialised countries is the peaceful and easy-going Portuguese life. Time means very little to anyone, from the flower-seller with a huge basket of flowers on her head, to the donkey standing patiently in the shafts of his cart loaded with all kinds of vegetables; from the fisherman mending his nets to the farmer behind his plough, gently encouraging his oxen.

Tomorrow will come—*se Deus quizer*. There is nothing you can do to hurry it up.

Schools and Universities

Although Portugal has one of the oldest universities in Europe —founded in 1290—education is still not very advanced when compared with the school, technical college and university systems of countries like Great Britain, France and Germany.

Since 1911, primary education has been compulsory, yet more than a quarter of the population above the age of seven is unable to read and write. This is because there are not enough state primary schools in the country districts, and also because many poorer families in towns where there *are* schools do not bother to send their children to school, although the state primary education is free. Up till now, the authorities have not been strict in seeing that young children attend school.

Another possible reason is that there are not enough state primary schools providing free education in the towns. There are private primary schools, just as there are private secondary schools. But these schools, the majority of which are church schools, charge fees which poorer families cannot afford.

The capital city of each province has a state secondary school and so do the next three important towns in each province. With those in Lisbon there are about forty state secondary schools altogether, which is not enough for the population of ten million people. Even state secondary education has to be paid for, though the fees are not so high as those in private secondary schools. There are 164 state technical schools, but only five art colleges throughout the whole of Portugal.

In 1290, King Denis founded the university of Lisbon. He was himself a poet and much interested in scholarship, though he was best known as the Farmer King. In 1537, the university was moved to Coimbra which, for a time, became the capital instead of Lisbon.

Coimbra is a beautiful city. The oldest part—the part where the university is situated—is built on the side of a hill, round the foot of which the River Mandego meanders. It was King John III who gave the beautiful palace, built by his father Manuel I, to house the students when he moved the university from Lisbon. John V, who reigned from 1706 to 1750 during one of Portugal's most prosperous periods, gave to the university a library which is the envy of many universities throughout the world. He built a beautiful building, consisting of three huge rooms, to house it. And he presented it with ten thousand manuscripts and books. Today the library has more than one million volumes.

Naturally, Coimbra "belongs" to the students. They have their own code of behaviour drawn up in "dog latin", which has many complicated rules. Woe betide any student who breaks one.

Although Coimbra is one of the hottest cities in Portugal, the students wear a black frock-coat and over the coat a short black gown. (They wear no hats.) Nowadays, the students are punished by civil law if they commit any misdemeanour, but in the past the university had its own courts and prisons.

Today, too, a student is rarely seen without his guitar. Coimbra is probably the one place in Portugal where you can still hear the real traditional *fado*.

The university year finishes at Coimbra in May. In great excitement the students then burn the ribbons which have been decorating their brief-cases throughout the year—a red ribbon for law, a yellow ribbon for medicine, a blue ribbon for the arts—and have a happy time feasting, singing and dancing, in which everyone is invited to join. It will not be their fault if you do not share their roast suckling pig, grilled sardines and other delicacies.

Among Coimbra's most famous students have been Portugal's greatest poet Luis de Camoens, who lived at the same time as Shakespeare (he died in the same year that Philip II of Spain seized Portugal, saying on his death-bed, "I am dying at the same time as my country"); and Dr. Antonio Salazar who, dictator though he was, certainly saved Portugal from economic disaster.

In 1911, a new university was founded in Lisbon, and another in Oporto, the second largest city. Since then, three others have also been founded.

The Portuguese authorities have been aware for a long time that their system of education is not sufficient for the needs of the country. In recent years, several attempts have been made to provide new schools, especially in the country districts, but such plans take a long time to take shape, and there is still *se Deus quizer* to take into account.

Lisbon and its Surroundings

One of the great rivers of Spain, the Tagus, empties itself into the Atlantic about a third of the way up the west coast of Portugal. On its right bank, at what is the most western point of Europe, on the slopes of a range of small hills, stands Lisbon, the capital of Portugal.

There has been a settlement at this spot for as long as mankind can remember. The Greeks, who traded along the coast of Portugal, had a legend that the first settlement here was founded by the great adventurer Ulysses. Certainly, for a long time the place was called Ulyssipona, but historians believe

The Lisbon suspension bridge which spans the River Tagus

that the Phoenicians set up a trading post there, and gave it the name Alis Ubo, meaning "the calm road-stead". The Romans called it Felicita Julia. They linked it with good roads to other fortified posts, built baths and a theatre and tried to make it as comfortable as they could.

The Goths added to it and built the first Cathedral. But it was the Moors, who invaded Portugal in A.D. 711, who first began to turn it into a really fascinating city, which they called Olissibona. Here they built splendid palaces and gardens. The name was changed to Lisboa—which we in turn, have changed to Lisbon—when the Moors were finally chased from the country in 1294. The name clearly is a shortened form of Olissibona.

Lisbon is a truly beautiful city. Its position above the great estuary of the Tagus makes it one of the most spectacular cities of Europe.

Round its tiled and many-coloured buildings is a belt of vines, parks, gardens and woods, broken here and there with villas, cottages and, surprisingly, farms; for the most important means of the livelihood of the Portuguese comes right up to and into the capital of the country.

There are two parts to the city. The old part, which was destroyed in the earthquake of 1755, and modern Lisbon, which not only contains the city which Pombal built after the catastrophe, but modern sections built during the Salazar era.

The oldest part is the Alfama, or eastern district, where

narrow winding streets crowd down to the river. Above them towers the castle, which the Moors began, but which is called St. George, in honour of the Portuguese-English alliance of 1386, since St. George is the patron saint of England.

In the "old" part of this city is the Sé, the ancient Cathedral which contains the tomb of St. Vincent. The Sé, which was built in 1147, was partly destroyed by the earthquakes of 1344 and 1755. Not far from it is the St. Vincent monastery which contains the tombs of the Portuguese Kings.

The central district of Lisbon, known as the Baixa, was built after the earthquake of 1755. It stretches from the river right up to the old district in the north. Its streets are wide and are laid down to a geometrical plan, broken up by large squares. The most central of these squares is the Terreiro do Paço. It was built by the Marquis Pombal, and is known as Black Horse Square, because in it stands the statue of King Joseph I on his horse. The Baixa is the commercial district of Lisbon. The Black Horse Square is called Praço do Comercio (Commerce Place) on the maps.

The Terreiro do Paço, Lisbon

The most modern part of Lisbon lies to the north. This was the part built at the end of the eighteenth century, when the city took on another of its new leases of life.

Lisbon first became important when its inhabitants asked John of Aviz to become Defender of the Realm, and later made him King, in 1385. In return for the people's trust in them, the Aviz family set out to make their city the richest city in the world. Thanks to the huge profits made from the spices brought back from the east after the route to India had been discovered, they succeeded.

This first development of Lisbon, reached its peak during the reign of Manuel I (1495–1521). Manuel spent more on beautifying the city than any other King, encouraging builders and sculptors, who produced a new style in their arts, known as the Manuelin style. This was the really splendid period of Lisbon's history, and from this time the people have retained their love of beautiful and precious things.

But as the influence of Portugal in the world waned and waxed, so the city was neglected or improved. The modern district represents one of the later periods of expansion, when it was decided that Lisbon had become too congested. Wide Streets—the Avenidas Novas, the new avenues—were laid out, in the style of Lisbon's most famous avenue, the Avenida da Liberdade, which was opened in 1880. Forty years later, another expansion took place, which brought into the city's limits many of the villages which lay on its northern fringe. The villages quickly disappeared, their places being

A view of Lisbon from the Castle of St. George

taken by airy streets, lined with apartment and office blocks. Many of the commercial offices of the Baixa were moved out to the new suburb, and Lisbon's airport has been built there, as well as sports stadiums, hospitals and schools.

However, in spite of all the expansion—Lisbon now has a population of well over a million—the new has not destroyed the old. The modern planners have kept Pombal's straight streets, used old roof tiles, and built many balconies, painting them all in soft colours.

In 1966, a feat which many said could not be done was successfully accomplished—a suspension bridge was thrown over the Tagus, which here is 3·2 kilometres (two miles) wide. It is the longest suspension bridge in Europe.

Because of the bridge, the new Lisbon is spilling across the river.

Besides being a city of narrow streets, wide avenues, broad squares and many beautiful parks and gardens, Lisbon has a charm which many other cities lack. Perhaps this is due to the old and the new being side by side in several districts of the city and blending so well. Perhaps it is because, even here in the capital, the pace is slower than in other great towns, and *se Deus quizer* is heard as much as in the country villages.

There are few European cities left now in which shoe-shine boys kneel at their boxes—and get custom; where knife-grinders push their "stones" along the streets, attracting attention with shrill tunes on their fifes; and where on street-corners there are pedlars crying their wares—figs, olives, sardines straight from the sea, preserved fruit, cakes, flowers. You will find them all over Lisbon.

In Lisbon, like the old and the new cities, the rich and the poor live side by side.

No matter in which direction you go outside Lisbon you are bound to come upon a place of interest (for one reason or another) within the hour.

The coast from the mouth of the Tagus north to Cape Carvoeiro is known as the Costa do Sol—the sunshine coast. If you take the motorway (which begins in Pombal Square) and go down to the coast road, you will soon reach the seaside towns. Although they are small, they have hotels, snackbars and shops, but nothing so blaring and brash as Spain's new resorts.

Presently you will come to Estoril, which is a really fashionable resort, attractive to Europe's exiled monarchs and the international smart set. Estoril has no history; it sprang up overnight early in the present century. In the casino, the centre of the life of Estoril, they talk of yachts, golf and bridge, and nowadays of backgammon, too. On tennis courts, immaculately dressed men and women try to work off the weight which has come from eating too well and drinking early and late. On the beaches, tanned bodies pay homage to the sun, having nothing better to do.

The beach at Estoril

The lighthouse at Cascais

Within a few minutes of Estoril, across the bay, is Cascais, the rival of Estoril and weighed down with history. In the sixteenth century, the infamous Spanish Duke of Alba beheaded the governor in the town square for daring to resist him. For centuries Portuguese kings and queens brought their families here for the summer holidays. The people of Cascais claim that one of their fishermen, Alfonso Sanches, discovered America ten years before Columbus. He met Columbus in Madeira and told him of his discovery, shortly before he died, and it was Alfonso's log-books that led the Genoese navigator to the New World.

But it is not a king or queen or Alfonso Sanches to whom the people of Cascais have put up a monument. They have

66

honoured in this way, Marshal Carmona, who was the first President of the Portuguese Republic. Carmona (who was President for twenty-two years) loved Cascais, its people, its sun and its coast. He spent as much time as he could living in the citadel, his favourite home.

If you take the road north from Cascais, you will come to Sintra, perched on the edge of the Serra de Sintra. Here are the finest country houses to be found anywhere in Portugal. Sintra is a very special place. On the Costa do Sol they claim that the sun shines all the year round. (It is a more genuine claim than the Algarve's.) But Sintra attracts the sea-mists, and even in summer it stays cool.

Sintra, they say, is an enchanted place. Perhaps it is, but if the Lisbon sky is grey, or the Sintra hill-tops are hidden in mist, or if the donkeys are braying ceaselessly, or you are feeling the least bit depressed—stay away! Rather than enchanted, it is bewitched. Only when the mists have rolled away, and Sintra opens up like a rose after the rain, is it wise to go there.

And arriving there, what do you find? Nature in all its beauty, magnificent views and three castles.

The oldest castle is the fortress built by the Moors on the hill-top to guard the valley below, but it is the Paço da Vila which has the most history. What the castle at Windsor is to English history, so the Paço da Vila is to the Portuguese.

Denis, the poet king (1279–1325) built the castle here "for his pleasure", but it was the House of Aviz which made the castle memorable. King John I gave his daughter Isabel to the powerful Philip of Burgundy at Sintra, and it was at Sintra that he was caught kissing one of Queen Philippa's ladies-in-waiting. Excusing himself to the queen, he insisted that the kiss was *por bem*—"of no account"—and she believed him. But the incident caused much gossip and, to get his revenge, John ordered a ceiling in the palace to be painted with as many magpies as the queen had gossiping ladies-in-waiting. Each bird has in its claw a red rose of Lancaster—Philippa was the daughter of John of Gaunt of England—and coming from its beak are the words *por bem*.

Alfonso V spent little time in Portugal, but he was born and died in the same bedroom in this castle. However, it was Manuel I who made the Paço da Vila the splendid place it is. On his travels in Spain he had admired the horseshoe windows, the sheen of glazed tiles, the tall chimneys, the sunlit fountains in the orange-scented courtyards.

These, however, did not suit the taste of Queen Maria, whose third husband, Ferdinand of Coburg, decided, in 1840, to change the old sixteenth-century monastery on Sintra's largest hill-top, into a new palace. Known as the Palacio da Pena, it is a patch-work of almost every style of architecture—Arab minarets side by side with Gothic turrets, baroque cupolas and onion-shaped Russian domes.

Taking the road from Sintra back to Lisbon, you will come to Queluz, where you will find what many consider the most attractive and romantic of all Portuguese royal palaces. Built in the middle of the eighteenth century by a Frenchman at the command of Prince Pedro, it was to replace the country house which had always belonged to the sons of the kings. Robillon, the architect, produced a beautiful miniature Versailles, all pink, standing in formal French gardens. It is now used as a guest-house for visiting kings, queens and presidents.

Crossing the suspension bridge to go south you come to the Costa da Caparica. An unbroken stretch of sunny beach makes the Caparica much safer than the Costa do Sol, whose beaches are often closed by huge Atlantic breakers. Here new resorts have sprung up and are attracting more and more visitors.

But you can never get away from the old in Portugal. The new resorts here rub shoulders with centuries-old fishing villages. When the boats come in at dusk, the catches are sold to the highest bidder, and much of the fish will be on sale in Lisbon next morning.

Fishermen on the beach counting their catches

In the Provinces

Estremadura is a narrow strip of a province, on the coast. It includes the Costa do Sol, and stretches north to the border with the province of Maritime Beira. The traditional road to the north runs through it, so it has a long history.

The southern part of Estremadura, nearest to Lisbon, consists mostly of the *terras saloias*—the rich market gardens which provide the capital with its fresh fruit and vegetables. The little gardens are carefully laid out and tended by hand, fat pumpkins sit on the roofs, and on every hill-top a windmill's sails go round.

In the midst of this simple agricultural countryside sits the huge monastery of Mafra. It covers 103,600 square metres (40,000 square yards) and was begun in 1717 as the result of

A Portuguese miller and his wife, with their mill in the background

a vow made by John V, should he be granted an heir. It is closely copied from Spain's Escorial, and it took 50,000 workers, eighteen years to finish.

Rich though the *terras saloias* are, to the north of Lisbon, Estremadura is hilly, rough and barren. Barely half of the whole province is cultivated. In the Tagus valley, wine, olive oil and fruit are produced. It has hardly any manufactures, but cork, salt and fish are exported.

In what is perhaps the most desolate part of the province, where only sheep and goats are reared, just outside the little town of Fatima, on 13th May 1917, the Virgin of the Rosary appeared to three young shepherds and asked them to pray for the peace of the world. She promised to appear again on the thirteenth of the following months, and did so until 13th October. The three shepherds were present at each appearance, as were growing crowds of people, many of whom came to scoff.

The cult of Our Lady of Fatima spread throughout the world, and especially Europe, which was in the worst stage of the First World War. Thousands of pilgrims began to arrive in Fatima to pray for peace and it was claimed that many miraculous cures took place. For a number of years, the pilgrims camped out, but in 1925 a fine church was built, and monasteries and hostels, where the pilgrims can stay. At the spot where the shepherds saw their visions stands the Chapel of the Apparitions, in which there is a beautiful statue of the Virgin.

From May to October, especially towards the thirteenth of each month, all the roads of Portugal are crowded with people making their way to Fatima, some in carts, some in buses, but many on foot. On the twelfth and thirteenth of May and the twelfth and thirteenth of October the great pilgrimages are held, but on the thirteenth of each month between these dates elaborate and impressive ceremonies take place.

THE RIBATEJO

The Portuguese name for the Tagus is the Tejo. There are two provinces named after it, one being the Ribatejo, which literally means the "banks of the Tagus".

Ribatejo meets the Tagus as it comes into Portugal from Spain, and goes down on either side of it until it reaches the sea. It is a region of vast plains, where the grass is so green it often looks blue.

This is the country of horses and of fighting bulls. The Portuguese, like the Spaniards, have for centuries made bull-fighting their main entertainment. But the Portuguese bull-fight, as practised today, is different from the Spanish. This is because when the House of Braganza came to power they objected to the brutality of the *corrida*, which fell out of favour, except with the daring gypsies who had a passion for these *festa bravas*.

On the other hand, fighting the bull was part of the Portuguese way of life, and a new kind of fighting was introduced —the *corrida* on horseback. This proved more dangerous for

72

the man than the bull. When in 1799, a prominent nobleman, the Count of Arcos, was torn to pieces in front of the Queen and all her court, the Queen pronounced that Portugal had not enough men to risk the life of a single one against that of a bull. From that time, balls were placed on the tip of each horn, held in place by a sheath, and it was forbidden to kill the bull in the ring.

The Portuguese *toreiro* (bull-fighter) still fights the bull on horseback, but the horses he uses are not the hacks of the Spanish bull-ring. They are thoroughbred stallions reared on the plains of Ribatejo, where they become accustomed to the smell and the galloping of bulls. Besides this, however, they are not only trained to answer to the slightest command, but are also taught a kind of *dressage*, which is performed in the parade before each fight begins.

As in the Spanish version, the matador, mounted, places darts in the bull's neck to weaken it. But at the moment when the Spanish matador would plunge his sword into the bull, the Portuguese matador makes only the gesture of doing so. He then salutes the crowd and rides off.

Immediately a team of men run into the arena. On foot, with no weapon in their hands, they go towards the bull. As they near the bull, their leader goes to one side, and challenges the animal to attack him. When it does, he seizes its horns and does a hand-spring. While the bull is thus distracted the other men grapple with it until it is exhausted. Then oxen are brought in and the bull is led away.

73

In the bull ring. Note the *toreiro's* magnificent costume

If he has fought well, he will be taken back to the plains to breed other bulls as brave as he is, since he will never fight again. Those that have not pleased, for one reason or another, are killed and their meat is given to the poor.

If you want to see the Portuguese bull-fight at its best, do not attend one in Lisbon, unless it is advertised as *antiga portuguesa* —"Portuguese old-style"—in which all taking part wear dazzling costumes and the horses wear rich trappings. Go instead to Vila Franca, just out of Lisbon, in Ribatejo.

MINHO AND THE DOUROS

The most northern province of Portugal is Minho, which is the gayest of all the provinces. The countryside is green and well

74

looked after; none of it is wasted. Vines twine round poplar trees and are trained to cross the roads to trees on the other side, so that you can walk through shady green tunnels.

The people take after their country. They work hard, but they play hard. Not a single summer Sunday passes in Minho, without a fair or a festival with processions and dancing. Even their work they turn into play. To see them picking grapes is to watch a ballet, the music to which they "dance" provided by their own songs. All of which is the more surprising since the people of Minho are among the poorest in Portugal.

Minho – local costume

To the east of Minho, is the province of Tras os Montes and Alta Douro, while to the south of it is the Douro Littoral (Douro on the coast). All three provinces are *the* grape-producers of Portugal. From the Tras os Montes vines come the grapes from which port wine is produced.

Port wine is one of the two wines most famous throughout the world, both produced on the Iberian Peninsula. (The other is the sherry of Spain).

Port takes its name from the city of Porto (or Oporto), where it is made. Porto is the second city of Portugal and calls itself the capital of the north. It has a long history. Henry the Navigator was born here, and here he planned his expedition against Ceuta. But to the foreigner Porto's chief claim to fame is its wine. Porto has been producing port wine for several centuries. In 1763, a trading agreement was made between England and Portugal, by which Portugal was given the first choice of English wool, in return for which England was given the first choice of port wine.

As a result, British merchants with their families soon began

A wine-cellar on a Portuguese vineyard

Terraced vineyards on the banks of the River Douro. (The city of Oporto is at its mouth)

to arrive and settle in Porto. Though they intended to stay for good, they kept their English way of life. They married among themselves, and sent their children home to be educated in England.

These merchants chose the grapes, watched over the preparation of the wine and eventually organised its shipping in casks to Britain, where it was bottled—and drunk in great quantities by the Victorians—and sent round the world to wherever Englishmen might be.

There is still rivalry between the great port wine companies, as strong now as two hundred and fifty years ago. The names of Sandeman, Cockburn and Croft, and the Portuguese Borges, Barros and Ferreira all mean just one thing wherever they are spoken—port wine.

Table wines are also made from the grapes of Tras os Montes and Douro. The grapes are still crushed by human feet, so that the pips are not crushed and in order to draw the most goodness out of their skins.

Wine, however, is not Porto's only means of livelihood. Each year, more than five million hampers of sardines are brought into the wharves of Leixoes, the artificial harbour built on the coast of the mouth of the Douro, because of the continual silting up of the estuary. Prepared and canned, they represent the major part of Portugal's great sardine export.

There is a Portuguese saying: "Coimbra sings, Braga prays, Lisbon shows off, and Porto works." Porto certainly works.

THE ALENTEJO

Alentejo means "beyond the Tagus". As one would expect from this, it is the province to the south of the river from Lisbon. In area it is about one quarter of the whole country; it is also the least populated.

In the past it shared with the Algarve the role of battlefield, first against the Moors, then against the Spanish invaders. Today, it is the storehouse of Portugal, from which come two-thirds of the world's production of cork, while large herds of sheep graze the plains and pigs in considerable numbers grow fat on the acorns of the cork oaks. Now that irrigation has been introduced to provide water (which the rivers, dried up by the fierce summer sun, do not), olive oil, rice,

Freshly picked oranges waiting at the roadside for transport

oranges and pine oil, as well as marble, add to the income of the Alentejo farmers.

Never go to the Alentejo in the summer. There is an old saying: "The Alentejo has no shade", and this is true. This has had the result that probably more so here than in any other part of Portugal, a man's house is his refuge—from the fierce heat of summer and the extreme cold of winter. In turn, this dependence on home has developed a people more closely knit in families than anywhere else in this country where the family is the centre of everyday life.

In spaces in the plains swaying with wheat, on the edges of cork forests and olive groves there are small hamlets, with perhaps a hundred families. The landowner not only owns the countryside as far as the eye can reach, he is also responsible for all who live on it. He looks after them when they are ill or disabled or old; his wife watches over the marriages and the births; attends the sick and gives advice and comfort.

But things are beginning to change. The young generation of Alentejos are hearing that there are easier ways of making a living than ploughing and sowing in the sharp ridges of shale which will not take modern agricultural equipment. As they leave, "foreigners" from other parts of Portugal come in to take their place. These newcomers, who may stay only one season, are upsetting the whole basis of family life. Soon none of the great farms of the Alentejo—with their "ranch" houses complete with chapel, the hundred hams in the smoking-shed, the thousand cheeses in the dairy—will remain.

In the new Portugal of the 1980s, who can say what will take their place?

THE ALGARVE

The Algarve is the most southern province of Portugal. It is the country of the almond trees, orange groves and fig trees—and of tourism. The Moors, who held this part of the country for five hundred years, turned it into a garden; it is the modern fashion for taking holidays abroad, that has turned its southern coast into a tourist attraction.

In the Algarve the influence of the Moors remains. Village churches have Moorish domes, the houses have thick walls and terra cotta tiled roofs in the Moorish fashion, and even today some of the older women still cover the lower part of their faces with a half-veil.

The Algarve's long coast-line produces some of the best seamen in Portugal, yet the majority of the people rely on the land for their living.

In the south-west corner of the Algarve is the Serra de Monchique, a small mountain range which rises to about 900 metres (2,950 feet) and comes right down to the sea to form the towering cliff of Cape St. Vincent. The drive up to the little town of Monchique from any of the coastal resorts is the best way to see the province.

On your way you will go through almond orchards and olive groves, and empty small villages—empty because their serious inhabitants, clad in black, are all working in the fields, orchards or groves. Making this trip from Albufeira, one can

An olive grove – a typical scene in many areas of the Portuguese countryside

drive for more than two hours without meeting another motor-car, and only passing slow-moving carts drawn by plodding oxen, and patient donkeys laden with produce.

Half-way up the pine-covered slopes of the *serra* you can stop at a *pousada* for a meal. A *pousada* is a guest-house run by the Portuguese government. The rooms are simply furnished with just the necessities, but they are comfortable, and the food is excellent—and all for a fraction of the cost in a simple hotel.

The government has a chain of about twenty-five *pousadas* up and down the country. Most are small, with between five and ten bedrooms, but those at Elvas and Estremoz are classed *de luxe*. The Estremoz *pousada* is in a castle, and with eighteen luxurious rooms is the largest of these inns. The only snag about a *pousada* is that you may not stay for more than three nights.

We have said that the southern coast of the Algarve is one long beach. Really it is a series of beaches, made by the short headlands which here and there jut out into the sea.

There is nothing much to choose between one resort and the next. Each has grown out of a little fishing village which has been there for centuries. Now, between June and September they are invaded by hordes of Scandinavian, British, French, Dutch, German and other sun-deprived northerners.

Madeira and the Azores

As mentioned earlier, Madeira and the Azores are both counted as provinces of European Portugal, though they are both more than 800 kilometres (500 miles) away—the Azores out in the Atlantic, west of Lisbon; and Madeira, south of Lisbon, off the west coast of Morocco.

Madeira is an extinct volcano. Shaped rather like a pear-drop, it is fifty-six kilometres (thirty-five miles) long, and twenty-one kilometres (thirteen miles) across at its widest, and it has an area of 797 square kilometres (308 square miles). About 267,000 people live there.

Besides the main island of Madeira, there are a number of smaller islands in the group. The largest, and only inhabited one, is Porto Santo, with a population of about 3,000.

A fishing and farming town on the north coast of Madeira

Madeira's capital is Funchal, whose harbour is seemingly bottomless, and so is able to accommodate large ocean-going cruise liners, which call in for a few hours' visit. Since the Second World War, however, the island has become a holiday resort for those who do not like the crowds which are found on the beaches of the Costa do Sol, the Algarve and the Spanish resorts.

The climate is better even than the Algarve's. The winter temperatures range between 18°C (65°F) and 27°C (80°F).

In these temperatures, tropical and subtropical plants and crops flourish. Fuschias cover the island with a radiance of colour all the year round; and sugar cane, cereals, grapes, bananas, and many other fruits are produced.

The centre of the island is a mountain range, whose highest peak rises to a height of 1,860 metres (6,102 feet). There are

A view of Funchal, the capital of Madeira. Its deep harbour can accommodate large liners.

no beaches, so the new villas and hotels have swimming-pools for their residents and guests.

Madeira produces two things of importance to Portugal—wine and sugar. Madeira wine is a blend of the juice of white and black grapes and was once a very "fashionable" wine in England, and other parts of Europe. Besides Madeira wine and sugar, bananas and pineapples are also exported.

The people of Madeira are the descendants of Portuguese, but there is also a mixture of Moorish and Negro blood. In country districts, both men and women wear the *carapuca*, a small cap of blue cloth shaped like a funnel, with the pipe standing upwards. The men wear linen trousers, drawn tight, ending just below the knees, with a coarse shirt covered by a short jacket.

Because the island consists of steep slopes, neither horses nor mules nor even donkeys are able to help in working the land. All must be done on foot.

The first people to come to the Azores (a group of nine small islands) were the Portuguese, who first arrived in 1432, and gave them their name—the Azores, meaning the Vultures. The islands cover altogether 2,388 square kilometres (920 square miles) and have a total population of about 320,000. The largest island is St. Miguel (1,165 square kilometres—450 square miles) and the smallest Corvo (twenty-one square kilometres—eight square miles).

The people of the Azores are a strong and hardy people,

for their homes are the meeting-place of cyclones and other violent storms. They go everywhere on the backs of mules, astride a sack of straw for a saddle.

The capital of the Azores is Ponta Delgada, on St. Miguel, which is called the "green island". In fact, it is greener than Ireland, but in Ireland you do not see the palm-trees, the windmills and the vineyards of the Azores, or the ancient wagons with huge wheels.

In the centre, St. Miguel is made up of mountains and valleys. The valleys are thickly forested. From cracks in the black rock steam billows, rising from hot underground

**A thickly forested valley
on St. Miguel**

The waterfront at Ponta Delgada

springs, which here and there bubble out next to icy waterfalls. At certain spots, it is possible to cook a chicken by wrapping it in a cloth and burying it in the volcanic ashes which are still hot.

Everywhere you go, no matter on which island, you will find the strangest mixtures of flowers and plants, all over-sized. Giant azaleas, cannas, hydrangeas and camelias, cornstalks, boxwood, ginkgo and monkey trees, palm and pine trees make you wonder if you are not in some strange world of science fiction.

The people of the Azores are Portugal's finest sailors and

fishermen, who use the whale much as the *toreiros* of Portugal use bulls. Lookouts on the cliffs, announce the arrival of a school of whales. At once the light boats are pushed out to sea. In the prow are men armed with harpoons (not harpoon *guns*) and before the whales know that they are being attacked, several of them have been harpooned. When the whale is dead, it is towed ashore and cut up, and its ambergris and spermaceti are extracted. The latter form a fine oil which, like the ambergris, is supplied to the cosmetics industry.

In recent years, the Azores have been turned into a tourist attraction. Santa Maria, St. Miguel and Terceira have air-fields, but to reach the other islands you must go by boat from one of these three. Comfortable hotels have been built on all the larger islands, and if you are a keen fisherman or like shooting (hares, partridge, woodcock and rock doves), or are a tennis player or golfer, you will find these pastimes prepared for you.

Portugal Overseas

The Portuguese empire was much older than the British, Dutch or French empires. It came into being as a result of the fifteenth-century voyages of discovery, when trading-posts were set up wherever Portuguese merchant ships called. It has also been the longest-lasting of these empires, for when the British, French and Dutch decided, after the Second World War, to give their colonies independence, the Portuguese stubbornly refused to do so.

Formerly known as Portuguese West Africa, Angola, which lies south of the equator, is bounded on the north and east by the Congo and Zambia, and on the south by South West Africa (Namibia) and Botswana. Its capital is Luanda, which is a fine port, and has a population of seven million, the great majority of whom are black Africans. It covers 1,245,790 square kilometres (481,000 square miles).

Angola's importance to Portugal was its rich mineral deposits. These included copper, iron, petroleum, asphalt, gold, lead, coal, diamonds, mica, manganese and sulphur.

In 1960 the Angolans began to demand independence, and guerilla movements, the chief of which were the MPLA and FNLA-Unita, came into being. For fifteen years, the Portuguese refused to give in, but after the revolution of 1974, the new government promised independence.

Fighting then broke out between the guerilla movements. The MPLA which was communist in outlook, was sent military advisers and arms by Soviet Russia, and soldiers by Cuba. FNLA-Unita received no help at all. It was not surprising, therefore, that the MPLA won, and a communist, independent Angolan government was set up early in 1976.

However, Unita is still a force to be reckoned with, and the future of Angola remains uncertain.

MOZAMBIQUE

Mozambique used to be known as Portuguese East Africa. It is bounded by Tanzania on the north, and Malawi, Zimbabwe and South Africa on the west. It has an area of 771,820 square kilometres (298,000 square miles). Its capital is Lourenço Marques, a very fine port, and it has another important port at Beira. It has a population of 12,200,000.

Unlike Angola it has few minerals, so far as it is known, but its importance to Portugal came from the dues paid for the transport of goods by other African countries, through Lourenço Marques and Beira.

When an independence movement was begun after the 1974 revolution, the Lisbon government promptly granted its demands.

GUINEA-BISSAU AND THE CAPE VERDE ISLANDS

Guinea-Bissau is the third African territory which once belonged to Portugal. It is situated on the north-west coast of Africa, and is bounded by Senegal on the north, and Guinea on the south-east. It is comparatively small, having an area of nearly 36,260 square kilometres (nearly 14,000 square miles) with a population of 800,000.

Except that it is not far from the Cape Verde Islands, which also once belonged to Portugal, it had little importance for the mother country.

GOA, DAMAN AND DIU

These small, widely separated territories in India, were once Portuguese colonies. All three are on the west coast.

Goa's chief claim to fame is that it was christianised by St. Francis Xavier; Daman is 112 kilometres (seventy miles) north of Bombay; while Diu is a tiny island with a piece of mainland on the coast of the Gulf of Cambay, opposite Daman.

In 1961, the government of India lost patience with Salazar who refused to give up these territories, and they sent in troops to take over all three.

LORO SAE

The third largest island of the Indonesian archipelago, and also the nearest of the whole group to Australia, is Timor. While the western region belonged to the Dutch and became a part of Indonesia when the Dutch gave independence to their East Indies, the eastern region was kept by Portugal, and in 1976 became part of the Indonesian Republic under the name of Loro Sae.

Macao is opposite to and about fifty-six kilometres (thirty-five miles) from the British possession of Hong Kong on the South China coast. Though very small—it consists of a peninsula and two small islands, with an area of about sixteen square kilometres (six square miles), and a population of 280,000—it is the most interesting of Portugal's possessions.

It was the Portuguese who opened up regular trade between China and Europe in 1516. Forty years later they established Macao, sending there one thousand Portuguese families. Today's inhabitants are descended from these original thousand families but, over the centuries, the Chinese have married with them, to the extent of producing a population that is now to all intents and purposes Chinese. So far, Macao has not asked for independence.

The Portuguese have never called their overseas territories colonies. They have always regarded them as provinces. Each is or was administered by a governor or a governor-general, who was helped by a council, two-thirds of whose members were or are elected. The governor-general is or was responsible to the Minister for Overseas Provinces in Lisbon.

Though the Portuguese colonies were granted independence by the new revolutionary government, Portugal can claim that her empire at least outlived all the other great empires.

The Revolution of 1974 and After

When a country has been firmly governed by one man, and that man an outstanding one, even a genius (however much you may not like the way he governs), unless it has a man of the same ability to take over when he dies, there is likely to be trouble.

Salazar had not trained a successor, and among those in the Portuguese government who might become prime minister, there was not one as outstanding as Salazar. One was not surprised, therefore, to wake up on 25th April 1974 and learn that the Portuguese Army had removed Prime Minister Marcello Caetano, and packed him off into pleasant exile in Brazil, and had announced that the Army was going to take over the government of the country.

Soldiers, however, with the possible exception of the Duke of Wellington, rarely make good politicians. Also, when a dictatorship is overthrown, the political parties which it has forbidden, but which have existed "underground", never seem ready to take responsibility without a good deal of squabbling.

Another point which nearly all (and especially military) organisations that overthrow governments do not seem to understand, is that if they really wish to govern for the good of *all* the people, they must reach agreement among themselves. The Portuguese Armed Forces Movement (MFA) did not understand this. They quarrelled among themselves and, because of this, they encouraged the political parties to quarrel amongst themselves as well.

An important faction of the MFA were Communist, and they naturally hoped that the Portuguese Communist Party would take over the government. As it has happened, the Communists were not able to win sufficient support to do this. From the latest election results, it seems that the Social Democrats and the Democratic Socialists are the parties most likely to bring peace and order to a country that is still a little unsure of itself.

The friends of Portugal—and there are millions—must wish that she will quickly solve her remaining problems.

Like these explorers on the Monument to the Discoveries at Belem, the Portuguese are looking forward to the future

Index

Seth, Ronald

Let's visit Portugal.